IMPROVING SPELLING
IN THE
MIDDLE GRADES

SECOND EDITION

Maryann Murphy Manning
Gary L. Manning

D1301748

nea PROFESSIONAL LIBRARY
National Education Association
Washington, D.C.

Note

The opinions expressed in this publication should not be construed as representing the policy or position of the National Education Association. Materials published as part of the Analysis and Action Series are intended to be discussion documents for teachers who are concerned with specialized interests of the profession.

Acknowledgments

The following materials are used with permission from the sources indicated:

Phonics rules for spelling from "The Applicability of Phonic Generalizations to Selected Spelling Programs" by Lille Smith Davis, *Elementary English* 49, no. 5 (May 1972), pp. 702-13; copyright © 1972 National Council of Teachers of English.

Lists of spelling words from pp. 247, 248-49, 217, and 218-19 of *Language Experiences in Communication* by Roach Van Allen. Copyright © 1976 by Houghton Mifflin Company. All rights reserved. No part of this work may be reproduced or transmitted in any form or by any means, electronic or mechanical, including photocopying and recording, or by any information storage or retrieval system, without permission in writing from the publisher. Reprinted by permission of the publisher.

Lists of spelling words from pp. 15-17 and 18-21 of *The Teaching of Spelling* by James A. Fitzgerald. Copyright © 1951 by Bruce Publishing Company.

"Stages of Spelling Development" from *Teaching Spelling* by Edmund H. Henderson, p. 41. Copyright © 1985 by Houghton Mifflin Company.

Library of Congress Cataloging-in-Publication Data

Manning, Maryann Murphy.
  Improving spelling in the middle grades.

  (Analysis and action series)
  Bibliography: p.
  1. English language—Orthography and spelling.
2. Spelling ability   I. Manning, Gary L.   II. Title.
III. Series.
LB 1754.M29 1986   372.6'32   86–21647
ISBN 0–8106–1695–5

CONTENTS

The Authors

Maryann Murphy Manning and Gary L. Manning are Professors of Education at the University of Alabama in Birmingham. They are also the authors of *Reading Instruction in the Middle School* and *A Guide and Plan for Conducting Reading (K–12) In-Service Workshops*, published by NEA; and the editors of *Reading K–12: The NEA In-Service Training Program*..

The Advisory Panel

Vivian Moon Arthur, English teacher, Grand County Middle School, Moab, Utah

Charles E. Gobron, sixth grade team leader, Neary School, Southborough, Massachusetts

Darlene R. Johnson, Reading Specialist, Dawes and Walker Schools, Evanston, Illinois

INTRODUCTION

Institutions in our world—schools, businesses, government agencies—expect correct spelling. Many people interpret poor spelling as a sign of poor education. Spelling is ranked by many people as one of the most important areas of learning in school. Societal demands require that we include spelling instruction in the school curriculum. There are, however, numerous points of view regarding what methods are effective for developing good spellers.

In this century much research has been done in the area of spelling, but only since the early 1970s have significant breakthroughs occurred to help us understand how children develop as spellers. Unfortunately, these understandings have not reached into actual classroom practice. A major reason for this is that most publishers of spelling programs have ignored these ideas when constructing their materials and most school systems rely primarily on such published programs. While it is true that many students are learning to spell with the present curriculum, there are many who are not.

Goals of a spelling program include developing independent spellers who can spell many words and developing writers who will edit their written communications. If these goals are to be met, then the writing process approach should be emphasized in the middle grades. In this process approach, students are given ample time each day to write. They select their own topics, write drafts, confer with one another and the teacher, edit, and publish.

In many elementary schools, teachers use a set of spelling textbooks for a given grade level. These programs usually provide word lists, activities for students, and suggestions for teachers. Some school districts and many states dictate a set number of minutes per day or week for spelling instruction. Using the limited materials and suggested time guidelines, teachers develop spelling programs for their students. What teachers decide to do in developing a spelling curriculum is a reflection of their knowledge of learning theory and their beliefs about how spelling is best learned.

What can teachers do to improve instructional practices? The first step is to review the recent developmental research and to examine their current practices. After comparing their instructional practices with spelling research, teachers can make decisions about continuing their practices or changing them. In this publication, alternative spelling views are presented to assist teachers in making these instructional decisions.

Conflicting views exist regarding these questions: (1) Should spelling be taught informally in the process of writing or should instruction be presented formally? (2) What should be the format of informal or formal spelling? The first two sections focus on these issues.

In this second edition, the reader can note several changes we have made. In Part I, we include new research and ideas that are more specifically focused on the middle grades. In addition, we have added new references to that section and to the annotated bibliography. We have extensively revised the informal spelling section of Part II. Other minor changes can be found throughout the publication. We hope this second edition will help you decide how to provide a meaningful and effective spelling program for your middle grade students.

Part I

SELECTED RESEARCH AND RECOMMENDED PRACTICES

Our understanding of how students develop as written language users has increased significantly since the early 1970s. Until then many of us thought students simply memorized words or made the appropriate associations between sounds and symbols. We also thought they read first and then began writing at a later time. It was common teaching practice to insist on correct spelling in children's earliest writing and to correct all spelling errors students made. Most of us meant well, doing only what we thought was best.

We wish we could go back and reteach our students from those years, using what we now know about how spelling develops. We now know that young students in the kindergarten and first grade invent spelling as they write by going through one level after another of being wrong, rather than by simply making associations of isolated sounds and letters. And, of course, some students reach the middle grades who are still at those early levels in their spelling development. The research of Read (22)* and later the extensive research of Henderson (11) and others provide new insights about spelling development.

It's important for us in the middle grades to be aware of the research concerning spelling development from these early levels to the level of correct spelling. Indeed, as we mentioned earlier, there may be middle grade students who are at those early levels.

There are different models showing the levels of spelling development such as Read (24) and Ferreiro and Teberosky (6). We present the Henderson (12) model to show how students range in their development as spellers (Table 1). As you can see, students in the middle grades usually range from stage two through stage five. Henderson (13) provides a number of ideas for teaching students to spell, basing the teaching on the students' stage of development.

Without question, students construct their own knowlege about how words are spelled, just as they construct all other knowledge. They go through one level after another of being wrong. As they increase their understanding of our writing system, they spell more conventionally.

Teachers can use a number of strategies to help improve students' spelling; however, those strategies must be appropriate for their level of

---

*Numbers in parentheses appearing in the text refer to the Bibliography beginning on page 43.

Table 1
STAGES OF SPELLING DEVELOPMENT

Age 1-7	Age 5-9	Age 6-12	Age 8-18	Age 10-100
Stage 1	*Stage 2*	*Stage 3*	*Stage 4*	*Stage 5*
	Letter	Within Word	Syllable	Derivational
Preliterate	Name	Pattern	Juncture	Constancies
Scribbles	Most sight words spelled correctly	Most sight words spelled correctly	Sight words may or *may not* be transferred to spelling performance	Sight words may or *may not* transfer
Identifies pictures				
	Invented spelling by letter name	Invented spellings honor short vowels and long vowel markers	Invented spelling errors occur at juncture and schwa positions	Invented spellings "most frequently misspelled"
Draws				
Imitates writing				
Learns letters				

development. For example, you would approach spelling for students in stage one very differently than for students in stage four.

We provide an annotated bibliography in this publication. These books should increase your understanding of spelling development and should give you ideas for appropriate spelling instruction strategies.

INFORMAL SPELLING PROCEDURES

Students become conventional spellers by extensive reading and writing, desiring to communicate with others through written language. Zuttell suggests students should be encouraged "to read and write extensively, and to test, evaluate, and revise, if necessary, their developing theories of how the spelling system works" (29). Teachers using an informal approach have several common characteristics. First, they understand spelling development, building on each student's developmental level. Second, they read to students and encourage students to read independently. Third, they help students understand the orthographic regularity of English spelling. Finally, they use a writing process approach as a regular part of the curriculum. Let us now explore how you might incorporate these ideas into your middle grade classroom.

Levels of Spelling Development

It is important to know the spelling levels of students, so that appropriate spelling instruction strategies can be used. A teacher could gain insight about how students spell by administering and analyzing the results of a spelling test made from a word list located in the appendix or by using words from a spelling series.

A teacher friend of ours gave a spelling test to her fifth graders, consisting of thirty words that were taken from a fifth-grade speller. In correcting the test, she found a wide range of spelling scores. One student missed all of the words while two spelled all of the words correctly. In between these two extremes, she found a variety of scores. However, most of her students scored above 60 percent.

Was the teacher surprised by seeing the wide range of spelling abilities in her fifth-grade class? No, because she realizes the wide range of spelling abilities that exists in most classrooms. In analyzing the individual papers, however, she gained additional insights about students' spelling which became useful in helping them improve their spelling. For example, she found no students at stages one or two. Even the student who missed all of the words was in stage three. In all, there were four students in stage three. She found eleven students in stage four, and the other thirteen students were in stage five.

This fifth-grade teacher realized the range of spelling abilities in her class; therefore, she tried to accommodate that range. In her school, she has to follow the general spelling curriculum, but she has flexibility in using it. For example, she used the suggestions we gave in the first edition of *Improving Spelling in the Middle Grades*. She used the words from several grade levels of her school's spelling series and made an individualized spelling kit. She implemented it as we suggested in the first edition and as we suggest in this edition. In addition, she used a writing and reading process approach in her class; therefore, students read and wrote on a regular basis. Indeed, the classroom was a community of readers and writers.

Importance of Reading

Students' word knowledge will increase if we read to them and if they read independently. Zuttell (30) emphasizes that improved word knowledge leads to improved spelling abilities. Teachers need to make sure that they give students time to read independently and that reading materials are interesting, appropriate, and available. Students should self-select their own books and should have opportunities to interact with the teacher and other students about their reading. Unfortunately, some teachers think that middle-grade students have outgrown the practice of teachers reading aloud to them. However, we know many middle-grade teachers who think otherwise. They read aloud often and regularly to their students and their students reap the benefits.

Orthographic Regularities in English Spelling

Chomsky states, "the conventional spelling of words corresponds more closely to an underlying abstract level of representation within the sound system of the language, than it does to the surface of the phonetic form that the words assume in the written language" (2). While two words may be phonetically different, their spelling and meaning may be similar such as *nation* and *nationally*. Chomsky goes on to say that English spelling does make sense, if viewed from an orthographic viewpoint rather than from a purely phonetic standpoint.

What does this mean to the teacher of spelling? Chomsky (3) suggests that teachers should help students to recognize and use the regularities that do exist. Students can be helped to make connections between the spelling of words such as *criticize* and *critical* in order to spell *criticize* with a *c* rather than an *s*.

The Writing Process

It's gratifying to realize that teachers throughout the country are incorporating the process of writing in their classroom. The ideas of Graves (10) and Calkins (1) have greatly influenced our own views of teaching writing. They outline three phases of writing: rehearsal, drafting, and revising. In rehearsing, the writer daydreams, outlines, reflects, researches, etc. The writer then writes a first draft, focusing on getting thoughts and ideas on paper. Revision enables the writer to clarify, to reorder, to expand and to extend certain elements, etc. The three phases overlap as writers move back and forth among them. Throughout the phases of writing, the writer interacts with the teacher and other students in the room. One important interaction is the scheduled writing conference with the teacher. Other important points to keep in mind in implementing the writing process approach are as follows: provide time to write each day, allow students to self-select topics for writing, have students share their writing with one another and respond to one another's writing, publish selected writing, and emphasize content, not mechanics. Indeed, a number of resources now exist that should be helpful to teachers wanting to implement this approach and we have included some of these in the annotated bibliography.

Why emphasize the writing process in a publication about spelling? Because spelling is only one of many processes a student uses when composing. Spelling must be kept in that context; that is, spelling is for writing. Teachers can help students improve their spelling by working with them in the context of students' own daily writing.

FORMAL SPELLING PROCEDURES

In a formal approach to spelling, students study lists of words and take tests on those words to determine if spelling mastery has been achieved. Some teachers conduct their formal spelling instruction in a traditional fashion, having all students in the class study the same lists of words and take tests on a weekly basis. Other teachers, realizing the great range of spelling abilities in each classroom, may use a formal spelling program but individualize assignments and procedures. In the 1950s, Tyler (28) and Horn and Otto (19) described the vast range in students' spelling abilities at all grade levels. These findings hold true today, and the span of the difference increases with each progressive grade level. Important findings of individualized formal spelling programs include readiness, time, sources for words, rules, test–study–test method, and self-correcting test method.

Begin a formal spelling program only when a child is ready to spell, both intellectually and emotionally. Read, Allred, and Baird (24) suggest that before beginning a formal spelling program students should

1. have a mental age of about 7½ years.
2. be able to enunciate words clearly.
3. see that words are composed of different letters.
4. have a beginning phonetic sense and recognize the common letter-sound correspondence.
5. have the ability to write and name all the letters of the alphabet correctly.
6. be able to copy words correctly.
7. be able to write their own names without copying.
8. be reading at a minimum of second grade level.
9. be able to write a few simple words from memory.
10. ask for words they need in writing and be able to express a few thoughts in writing.
11. demonstrate an interest in learning to spell.

If characteristics of individual children are not considered before starting a formal spelling program, students may develop poor attitudes toward spelling that are difficult to change. If this list of criteria were carefully adhered to in the primary grades, some second graders and even some third graders would not receive formal instruction in spelling. Teachers can work with colleagues, administrators, and parents to gain support for beginning formal spelling instruction at different times for different students.

Implement short, highly motivating lessons rather than longer sessions since long periods of instruction each week do not increase spelling competence. Some people have been encouraging longer periods of spelling instruction time; however, Jarvis (20) reports that short sessions are more beneficial than longer ones. He suggests it may not be necessary to spend 75 minutes per week. Sessions need to be short and highly motivating because long sessions tend to become boring and less effective. The key to the number of minutes students spend on spelling should be the interest they exhibit.

Use high-frequency words and the child's own writing as sources for spelling instruction. Lists of spelling words often come from research studies of high-frequency words used by children. The better known of these studies include Dolch (5), Rinsland (25), Horn (14), and Fitzgerald (7).

Thomas Horn (16) notes that spelling is probably improved most by stimulating and attending to children's writing. However, he points out that research shows direct instruction with the high-frequency words is needed. While there are many suggested substitutes for the formal word lists, as Horn reports, many children need direct instruction with high-frequency words.

Most formal spelling series published in recent years have utilized high-frequency words in their word lists. Spelling series vary in the way that lessons are constructed and in the number of words presented. Words from a spelling series can be a good source for a word list. In the section on individualizing programs, we will describe a plan for the use of spelling series word lists as a part of an individualized program.

In addition to spelling series, there are numerous other word lists available. Lists and references to lists are included in the Appendix and the Annotated Bibliography. Suggestions for the use of these word lists are also given in the section on individualizing.

Teach only a few rules and use the recommended practices for teaching those rules. Conflicting views exist about what rules to present and how to present rules. Published spelling programs vary; some include many rules, others have a minimum number.

Students should not be asked to memorize rules, and time should not be wasted on rules if the student already can spell the words. If it is deemed necessary to teach a rule, it should be done inductively rather than deductively. A meaningful time for teaching a rule is in a teacher-student conference setting when proofreading is occurring. A short discussion of the words like the one misspelled, allowing the students themselves to discover the generalization, is far better than teaching rules when the students do not see the need for a rule.

12

In 1934, Foran (9) gave the following suggestions regarding rules and many people feel they still apply:

1. Teach only a few rules and include only those that have no or few exceptions.
2. Teach a rule only when there is a need for it.
3. Teach rules inductively rather than deductively.

Davis (4) suggests these phonics rules are applicable 100 percent of the time in spelling:

1. When *c* and *h* are next to each other, they make only one sound. *(torch)*
2. When the letter *c* is followed by *o* or *a*, the sound of *k* is likely to be heard. *(vacant)*
3. When *ght* is seen in a word, *gh* is silent. *(light)*
4. When a word begins with *kn*, the *k* is silent. *(knee)*
5. When a word begins with *wr*, the *w* is silent. *(wreck)*
6. When a word ends in *ck*, it has the sound as in *look*. *(track)*
7. When *ture* is the final syllable in a word, it is unaccented. *(venture)*
8. When *tion* is the final syllable in a word, it is unaccented. *(election)*
9. When the first vowel element in a word is followed by *th*, *ch*, or *sh*, these symbols are not broken when the word is divided into syllables and may go with either the first or second syllable. *(feathers)*

Additionally, Davis reports that these generalizations are applicable in spelling 77 to 99 percent of the time:

1. If the only vowel letter is at the end of a word, the letter usually stands for a long sound. *(spy)*
2. The *r* gives the preceding vowel a sound that is neither long nor short. *(orbit)*
3. Words having double *e* usually have the long *e* sound. *(teeth)*
4. In *ay* the *y* is silent and gives *a* its long sound. *(display)*
5. When *y* is the final letter in a syllable it usually has the sound of long *i*. *(cycle)*
6. When *a* is followed by *r* and final *e*, we expect to hear the sound heard in *care*. *(share)*

13

7. *Ch* is usually pronounced as it is in *kitchen, catch,* and *chair,* not like *sh.* *(merchant)*

8. When *c* is followed by *e* or *i*, the sound of *s* is likely to be hard. *(crease)*

9. The letter *g* often has a sound similar to that of *j* in *jump* when it precedes the letter *i* or *e*. *(age)*

10. In most two-syllable words, the first syllable is accented. *(quarter)*

11. If *a, in, re, ex, de,* or *he* is the first syllable in a word, it is usually unaccented. *(decide)*

12. In most two-syllable words that end in a consonant followed by *y*, the first syllable is accented and the last is unaccented. *(candy)*

13. If the first vowel sound in a word is followed by a single consonant, that consonant usually begins the second syllable. *(eager)*

14. When there is one *e* in a word that ends in a consonant, the *e* usually has a short sound. *(zest)*

15. When the last syllable is the sound *r*, it is unaccented. *(under)*

Use the test–study–test method which is proven to be most effective with intermediate grade children and the preview–test–study–test method in the primary grades. Fitzgerald (8), Thomas Horn (17), and Sherwin (26) report that intermediate students should use a test–study–test method and that primary students should use a preview–test–study–test method. Translated into practice this means that intermediate students should be tested on a list of words and then practice or study only those words that they misspell. After study, they again are tested. Both tests should be immediately corrected by the students themselves.

In the primary grades, the method is the same except for the preview step. Before students are tested, they look at or preview the words. Other parts of the book provide suggestions for alternative study methods and testing procedures.

Ask students to correct their own tests. E. Horn (15) and T. Horn (18) reported several decades ago that having students correct their own tests is an effective way to improve spelling. Some teachers express concern that some students will not check their words honestly or accurately. This problem may be minimized if teachers give special assistance to less independent students and help them learn to correct their tests accurately. Some students might be tested by the teacher at sample intervals.

Part II
ALTERNATIVES TO TRADITIONAL SPELLING PROGRAMS

A variety of spelling methods exists, allowing for alternatives as spelling instruction is planned for students. Informal and formal approaches are discussed in this section.

INFORMAL APPROACH TO SPELLING

An alternative to a formal spelling program is the informal approach to spelling instruction in which spelling permeates the entire curriculum. The resources used are inexpensive and relatively simple to assemble, and the activities are informal. The role of the teacher in the informal approach changes from the traditional caller of word lists to that of cooperative editor.

What Is Necessary?

Most of the resources needed are already in most classrooms: word lists, individual student word lists, dictionaries, spelling games, and writing materials. We have included several lists in the Appendix for reference; however, other word lists are readily available. These lists can be presented in a spelling center in numerous ways. They provide easy reference for students in their spelling and writing. This method departs from the traditional use of the list where all students were assigned specific lists with prescribed expectations for mastery. Individual student lists may be constructed by the student, by teachers in cooperation with the student, or by pairs of students. The lists may include words the student knows how to spell, words the student has difficulty in spelling, or both. In the initial stages of spelling study we recommend using words the student already can spell; however, as the students progress in their spelling, they should be given a choice as to which types of words will be most beneficial to them.

Dictionaries

Dictionaries appropriate for the developmental levels of the students are included in the spelling center. Glossaries and thesauruses should be included in intermediate and middle school level centers.

Spelling Activities

The spelling center can contain a collection of activities—commercial, teacher-made, and student-made. Examples are puzzles, "Scrabble for Juniors," alphabet blocks, and spelling games. Ideas for these activities are provided in the Spelling Activities section of this publication.

Activities are used for studying the words. In an informal approach, the activities could be used on a student self-selection basis. In a more formal approach, teachers contract with students, having them do a certain number of spelling activities during a given length of time. An example of a contract is to list five spelling activities and to contract with the student to complete two of the activities during a one-week period.

Writing Materials

The spelling center contains all of the items necessary for writing, such as paper and pencils, materials necessary to make dictionaries, word rings, book covers, and the like. The materials should be easily accessible for student use.

Reading and Writing Promote Spelling

Much reading and writing occur in classrooms when an informal spelling approach is used. Moffett and Wagner (21) suggest that students develop visual images of both regular and irregular words through reading, and this strengthens their spelling. They also believe that much writing practice is necessary for developing good spellers. As students are encouraged to write and students who are really extending their composing abilities make guesses at spelling as they express their creative thoughts, penalties for misspelling must be removed.

Editing

Editing can take several forms. There is self-correcting, peer-editing, and teacher-student editing. The goal of each is to develop independent spellers who edit their own writing. To reach this goal, set aside a place in the classroom for students to edit together and for teachers and students to edit cooperatively. In intermediate and middle schools, students can consult each other more often than the teacher.

A Problem

The one problem that often arises in classrooms where teachers utilize an informal approach is grading. Grading presents a challenge because there are no weekly lists with number grades and regular daily activities for all students in a classroom. There are no easy solutions to this problem, and this difficulty does prevent many teachers from using the informal approach. It may be possible for teachers to function with this approach in spelling throughout the entire curriculum and still comply with the school policy by having a short traditional spelling period and spelling tests. Teachers dedicated to using an informal approach in the teaching of spelling must come to grips with this serious issue and find a method that works for them in their schools.

Spelling in the Content Areas

Spelling words can be taught to intermediate and middle school students through content areas. Much of the spelling instruction in the content areas is done in an indirect manner. When vocabularly words are being presented for new concepts, the words are usually presented in some visual manner, such as on the chalkboard. Students are usually involved in writing the new words as they complete learning activities on the new concepts. Students can be assisted in spelling the new words either by verbally helping them, by providing lists of words, or by assisting students in the use of reference materials that contain the correct spelling.

Content area teachers can also help students with their spelling by requiring much reading and writing. Besides the writing, students' work can be improved through self-editing, peer-editing, and teacher-student editing. Another procedure teachers use is making dictionaries and glossaries readily available for students to use in the editing process. As content area teachers assist students in developing reading skills, they should assist in developing spelling skills, too.

INDIVIDUALIZED APPROACH TO FORMAL SPELLING

Teachers can develop their own formal individualized spelling programs which can reflect recommendations of spelling authorities and enable them to operate within the constraints of their own teaching situations. Ideas offered here regarding the use of word lists and student contracts provide both structure and opportunities for individualization.

Using Word Lists

In developing a spelling program with word lists, teachers may use the following steps: (1) develop the necessary word lists, (2) assemble spelling practice activities, (3) implement the teacher-made spelling program, (4) evaluate the program for constant improvement.

There is no one right way to individualize spelling programs. Since teachers and students differ in the way they work and each learning setting is different, teachers can try one way and continue to modify it to meet the particular class or situation.

Step 1. Develop the Necessary Word List

Word lists can be developed from two major sources. The first source, probably the most beneficial and also the most complex to manage, is misspelled words from individual student's work. The second source is lists that have already been developed in a spelling series. A good procedure is to combine the two, using a list of words in combination with words misspelled by the student.

The student's own words. Use a variety of ways to collect a student's own problem words. Words that students use and need to spell will emerge as they engage in functional or creative writing. Students can keep a list of these words as they discover the need to master them. Some children will find this easy to do while others may need constant reminding.

Word lists. Word lists that are already developed come from several sources. One source is publications like this one. Many language arts books contain word lists that may be organized in different ways: (1) words with similarities (word families); (2) graded lists (easy to more difficult); (3) spelling demons (words that are difficult to spell). Another method to use in developing a word list is choosing words from any spelling series.

Making the lists ready for student use. There are many ways to organize lists for student use. Short lists on index cards set up in kits can be very useful. Some teachers find that typing the words with a primary typewriter is the most legible method; others print the words with markers or pens. When the list is graded like those found in spelling series, the cards can be filed in a box from easiest to most difficult.

Step 2. Assemble Spelling Practice Activities

The teacher then assembles practice activities to help students learn to spell words. Activities can be taken from language arts books, other idea books, and articles from professional journals. Numerous activities are listed in Part III of this book.

After activity ideas are collected, they can be put on cards with directions explaining their use to the student. If the information is written at the student's reading level and the directions are clear, the student can do the activity without the help of the teacher. Laminating the activity cards increases their longevity.

Step 3. Implement the Teacher-made Spelling Program

After selecting or developing a spelling list or assembling activities and list, the program is ready for implementation. The role of teachers in this program is new to some. No longer will they stand in front of the room pronouncing spelling words. Time is spent on conferencing with students on work that has been completed, proofreading work, and encouraging. Some time may be spent pronouncing or dictating words, but not with large groups. Most work is done with pairs or individuals and only on a periodic basis. Moving from student to student or pair to pair, the teachers guide students to become more independent and proficient spellers.

Guides for Implementation

Guide 1. Assign appropriate spelling lists to students.

Guide 2. Pair students for instruction.

Guide 3. Develop a place and a system for students to record their progress on tests and activities.

Guide 4. Set up testing procedures.

Guide 5. Spot-test and confer with individual students.

Guide 1. Identify student's needs and assign to appropriate list. Students should work in the kit at levels where they can succeed. If the list is a graded one, a pre-test can be developed to place students appropriately by selecting a few words from various lists and developing level tests. Once students are placed, teacher observation can give clues about the appropriateness of placement. If many words are missed consistently, the placement is probably too high, and the student should be placed at a lower level. On the other hand, if the student is missing no words, placement is probably too low, and the student should be placed at a higher level or should quickly proceed through the lists until more appropriate lists are reached.

Guide 2. Pair students for instruction. There are several different methods of organizing pair learning. The teacher can examine and try different ones to see what will work best for each student. Some methods of pairing include (1) self-selection, (2) sociogram selection, (3) mixed achievement level pairing, (4) equal achievement level pairing.

Self-selection methods allow students to choose the person with whom they want to work in spelling. They remain paired as long as they wish or as long as the teacher determines that it is a successful pairing.

Sociogram selection is a more formal type of pairing where students are asked to write their first, second, and third choices of other students with whom they would like to work. The teacher then pairs students honoring as many first choices as possible and trying to pair each student with at least his/her second or third choices. Just as with informal self-selection, there may be students who are not selected, and it then becomes necessary to make assignments.

Mixed achievement pairing involves pairing students together who have different achievement levels in spelling. Some teachers like this because they feel the better speller can help the poorer speller.

Equal achievement level pairing pairs students who are at the same level in spelling. Some teachers like this because they feel these students can challenge one another and progress at optimum speed.

How do we begin with pair-learning and avoid problems? Try beginning with just a few students, perhaps the higher-achieving or more independent learners. The number of students paired can increase as the system gets under way. Some teachers institute the entire spelling program through pairing while others utilize pair-learning along with some group activities. Since pair-learning, or any form of organization where students are interacting with one another, is noisier than traditional spelling instruction in which only the teacher speaks as she or he pronounces words to students, it is necessary to maintain an orderly learning environment. Students learn to work together because pair-learning is an effective way to help individualize spelling. Students can help one another at their levels, and self-concepts of students may be improved through helping others. Through this interaction, motivation for spelling can be enhanced. Simply stated, pair-learning works!

Guide 3. Develop a place and a system for students to record their progress on tests and activities. Use a central location (a desk, counter top, table) for individual student folders containing assigned spelling activities, records of students' progress, and samples of students' work. In this same area, place the formal word lists in kit form.

Records in spelling are of two types: teachers' records and students' records. We do not advise teachers to display publicly the results of students' work with systems such as starred charts for perfect spellers or bar graphs informing observers who are the good spellers and poor spellers. Rather, teachers can have students record their own progress, and thereby chart their own spelling growth.

No one form is better than another. Several forms are included so that teachers may decide which will work best in their own situations.

FORM 1

MY SPELLING WORK

Card Completed _____ Day _____ My Score _____

_____

_____

_____

_____

_____

FORM 2

Student Name _____

List No.	Practice Activity No.	Number Correct	Date	Test Score	Partner's Initial

FORM 3

MY SPELLING RECORD

Name _____

List No. _____ Number Correct on pre-test _____

_____

Number Correct on post-test _____

Signature of Partner _____

FORM 4

INDIVIDUAL SPELLING PROFILE

Codes to match the 36 units found in most grade level spelling texts
with the letters representing spelling tests across grade levels. Student
checks or writes in the date in each cell when each level is mastered.

Name	A	B	C	D	E	F	G
1							
2							
3							
4							
5							
6							
7							
8							
9							
10							
11							
12							
13							
14							
15							
16							
17							
18							
19							
20							
21							
22							
23							
24							

Name	A	B	C	D	E	F	G
25							
26							
27							
28							
29							
30							
31							
32							
33							
34							
35							
36							

Guide 4. Set up testing procedure. Students administer pre-tests of appropriate word lists to their partners. If mastery is demonstrated, the student proceeds to the next list. If mastery is not shown, the student practices until the test is given again. The pair determines when the student is ready to take the test again. What is mastery? Mastery of a word list means to spell *all* the words correctly. However, if a student consistently misspells a particular word or two on a list, she or he should be allowed to move on to the next list and continue to review those misspelled words until mastery is achieved.

Guide 5. Spot-test and confer. Sometimes it is necessary to spot-test some or all of the students. Spot-testing is testing a student over a list of words selected from the lists the student has completed. This could be done as the need arises, such as when a student seems to be progressing through lists faster than the teacher thinks is reasonable. Spot-testing can also be done on a systematic basis; students might be regularly spot-tested after they have completed ten lists of words.

When students report they have mastered words and a teacher finds they have not, the teacher may quietly but firmly tell the students that these lists will not be recorded as mastered and that they must continue to work on them until they are mastered. Spot-testing uncovers students' inaccurate reporting of mastery and enables the teacher to learn who needs regular spot-testing and who can proceed without close attention.

Conferencing can also be done on a scheduled or informal basis. No matter how good the spelling kit, the practice activities, the teacher's management, or the pair-learning are, students need personal contact with teachers. Conferences achieve this. Students who are progressing well need to know that we teachers are aware of their progress and we encourage it. Students who are not progressing can be given encouragement and reinforcement in the conference.

No rule governs the frequency or length of the conferences. The time and frequency of conferences will be determined by variables such as the number of students and their individual needs. Some conferences may last three minutes, while others may last ten. Conferences can take place during the language arts period or at any time the teacher finds appropriate.

Step 4. Evaluate Program for Constant Improvement

Evaluation should be continuous. Individual teachers have different styles, and quality instruction can occur in different ways. Teachers may ask themselves these questions while working with a formal spelling program:

1. Are students working on words that are at their levels?
2. Are students succeeding in the spelling program?
3. Are students developing positive attitudes toward spelling?
4. Are students transferring their abilities to spell the list words to their writing?
5. Am I devoting an adequate amount of time to spelling, ensuring success, and avoiding boredom?
6. Am I careful with the rules I present and the way that I present them?
7. Am I presenting words in oral and written contexts?
8. Am I continually building the spelling resources available to students in my classroom?
9. Am I continually extending my management ability so that I can better meet the needs of more students?
10. Am I a model of one with a good attitude toward spelling?

Students' attitudes toward spelling are very important, and the success they feel in spelling influences these attitudes. While students will not always relate how they feel, an attitude inventory might give some clues. Try using the following inventory or modify it and develop your own:

INVENTORY OF SPELLING ATTITUDES

The best thing about spelling is _____

I know my teacher likes spelling because _____

The hardest part of spelling is _____

The thing I do not like about spelling is _____

I would be a better speller if _____

It is fun in spelling when _____

The best speller I know is _____

We have spelling in school because _____

When you grow up you use spelling to _____

People who cannot spell are _____

The thing that helps me most in spelling is _____

Student Contracts

Contracts may be used to involve students in making decisions about what they are to do, how they will do it, and how they will evaluate the outcomes. Student contracts have different uses and they can be employed along with teacher-developed word lists, commercial spelling materials, or the total curriculum approach.

Some teachers may want to use a contract with only a few students rather than an entire class. Several contract forms are provided which teachers can use if they wish to do student contracting in spelling.

FORM 1

SAMPLE CONTRACT

I _____

will do the following spelling activity before _____

_____

_____

_____

_____   _____
Teacher   Student

FORM 2

SAMPLE CONTRACT

Student Name _____

Starting Date _____   Ending Date _____

I will complete the following spelling before _____

Activity	Date Completed	Evaluation

_____
Student Signature

_____
Teacher Signature

FORM 3

SAMPLE CONTRACT

Name _____

List or unit number _____

Completed activities number 1 and 2.

Choose two additional activities from this list to complete:

1. Pronounce all words to a friend.

2. Use all words in a sentence. Have a friend listen.

3. Write a short story using at least seven words from the list.

4. Write a short play using five of the words.

5. Write sentences with ten of the words.

6. Look up the origin of three of the words.

7. Construct a crossword puzzle using five of the words.

My Work Record

Activity	Date	Self-Evaluation

Teacher	Student

Improved Use of Commercial Materials

The use of commercial materials can be improved by having students self-pace themselves in the commercial spelling books or by using a commercially prepared spelling kit.

Self-pacing in the Commercial Spelling Books

A spelling kit can be made by cutting up spelling textbooks. Cut up two spelling textbooks at each level using several levels of a spelling series. Two copies of each book are necessary because one side of each page is covered when the page is mounted. The pages, once mounted, can be placed in a box or plastic tube in a file order system from the easiest level to the most difficult. If students are asked to do the textbook activities suggested on the cards in addition to studying the words, make teacher's editions with correct responses available so that students can check their own work. Rather than removing the pages of the spelling books, some teachers copy the words from each unit on separate index cards. All levels of the series should be utilized; but, if this is not possible, use books at least one grade level below and one grade level above, in addition to the book at the grade level of the students.

When commercial spelling books are used to develop a spelling kit, the kit can be implemented in accordance with the suggestions given in the section on using word lists.

Commercial Spelling Kits

Commercial spelling kits have appeared on the market in recent years. Their quality varies, and some are designed as a total spelling program while others are supplemental to one specific series.

When considering the purchase of a commercial kit, teachers should ask the following questions:

1. Does the kit include both spelling lists and practice activities?
2. Is the kit multi-leveled and are the levels appropriate for my students?
3. Does the kit reflect spelling research?
4. Is the management system one that I can implement in my classroom?
5. Does the kit include a recordkeeping system?
6. Is the kit consumable?

Some kits provide spelling practice activities as well as lists of words. Good practice activities can provide students with attractive ways to learn words. An advantage of most commercial kits is that they do provide—in one box—a wide range of spelling words. The management system of a kit needs to be examined to determine if it can be implemented with ease. If teacher-aides or volunteers are required for successful implementation, the teacher should consider this before purchase. The time required to implement the program and the in-service training required must be considered also. Commercial kits should contain appropriate recordkeeping systems, since students will keep some of their own records.

A FINAL NOTE

Most teachers have their pet peeves about instructional practices in spelling, and we have ours. We believe the use of spelling bees and the use of spelling wall charts with rows of gold stars should be eliminated. Nothing damages students' ultimate success in spelling as much as sitting, for what seems like hours, after they have been eliminated, while others demonstrate their abilities in a spelling bee; or having a large chart visible to the world that tells everyone that certain students are poor spellers because they failed to get gold stars or 100 percent by their names. In addition, we believe giving spelling grades is a detrimental practice. When students are at one developmental stage and simply cannot make sense of conventional spellings because those spellings conflict with their hypotheses of how to spell words, their confidence in their own abilities as spellers is reduced. Therefore, if possible, spelling grades should be eliminated or at least minimized.

We hope that through reading the ideas presented in this section teachers will examine their spelling programs and some will possibly modify them. We hope other teachers will continue their practices because they find support for and success in what they are currently doing.

Part III

SPELLING ACTIVITIES

The use of the numerous commercial and teacher-made spelling activities available should be governed by the needs of the students and the value the teacher places upon such activities. Here are a few simple guidelines to use in choosing and developing spelling games and activities:

1. Keep games simple. Often spelling games become so complex that students lose sight of why they are playing the game.

2. All students in a small group should be actively involved in the game.

3. Students should work on spelling activities or games in pairs or small groups so they can capitalize on each other's spelling knowledge.

4. Students should write spelling words rather than spell the words orally. Writing helps students develop the correct visual image.

5. Competitive games should only be played with students of similar abilities. Only in children's stories should rabbits and turtles compete.

6. Checking for the correctness of the spelling should be a natural part of any spelling activity.

7. Spelling activities should always be success-oriented.

Spelling can be fun and need not be painful for students. Games, if self-selected and self-correcting, are usually a source of enjoyment.

While enjoyable and useful for many students, the following activities are intended to serve only as guidelines for teachers and can be modified in any way to meet the needs of the individual classroom and teacher. A spelling resource file of activities helps to keep the activities available to serve needs for a long period of time. This file of activities can be placed in a spelling center for maximum utilization.

Puzzles

Crossword puzzles and other word puzzles are available from many sources. They appear in paperback books that can be taken apart and laminated. Puzzles can be found in students' weekly newspapers and commercial kits; these can be mounted on cardboard and laminated. These puzzles contribute to building vocabularies, also.

Charades

Pairs of students and small groups can play spelling charades. This involves telling the number of letters in the word to be spelled and then acting out or pantomiming the word for the other team. In addition to spelling practice, students dramatize nonverbally.

Affix Team Competition

Small groups of students or pairs take a suffix, prefix, and/or root word. Within a prescribed number of minutes they compile a list of all the words they can think of or that they can find in the dictionary that include the affix or root word. As with most spelling activities, there is vocabulary-building potential in this game also.

Homophone Fun

This game is played by an individual, pair, or small group. Students search for words that sound alike but are spelled differently. Using the dictionary and asking others for suggestions are legal and encouraged. The emphasis is on producing the list and not on originality.

Scrabble for Juniors

This game has been published in very simple to very sophisticated forms. Poor spellers often do not like Scrabble, especially when points are given only for correctly spelled words. Teachers can allow students to make up their own rules for Scrabble, the purpose of the game being the practice. Many students, including the weaker spellers, enjoy the game if they feel free to use the dictionary.

Making Words from Words

Certainly an old activity but still a useful one is taking long words and constructing numerous words from all of the combinations. The long word can be one the students suggest, sometimes the name of an approaching holiday or new content area words. Have students work in pairs checking the spelling of words together.

Spelling Demon Games

Many commercial games are available to teach spelling demons such as "their" and "there." These games include board games and card decks. Use these games only if they fit the suggested guidelines and include high-frequency words.

Technological Devices

Many devices give students instant feedback on the spelling of words. The best of these devices give visual practice in recognizing the correct spelling of the word.

Spelling in Context

Make enjoyable spelling activities by taking humorous short stories and poems and deleting occasional words, leaving enough words for students to comprehend the meaning. Short fables and familiar nursery rhymes are good. An example is, "Mary had a l __ __ __ __ __ lamb."

Constructing Silly Stories

Rather than asking students to repeatedly write sentences with a spelling list, ask them to write a silly story using all words on the list. Often the humor will be clear only to the writer.

Dramatizing Spelling Words

Students enjoy spontaneous opportunities to dramatize words and their meanings. When the words to be dramatized are printed on cards, students develop visual memory of the words.

Anagrams

An anagram is a word that is made by changing the letters of another word. Some examples are: smile–miles, meat–team, pin–nip, saw–was, and run–urn. Games based on such visual wordplay can be motivating.

Computer Software

Activities for learning spelling patterns and conventional spellings are available in computer software. Teachers must be discriminating when they select spelling software, and also when they make decisions about time students spend at the computer, deciding that computer time is more valuable than actual reading or writing time for improving the students' spelling.

Editing Activities

Numerous editing activities are beneficial as spelling activities. One activity is asking students to compile a list of all the words they misspell over a short period of time. Students are then asked to group the words to determine if they can gain insight about their spelling of words.

In another editing activity, students who have personal copies of dictionaries are asked to place a small dot by all words that they look up in the dictionary The student then compiles a list of words looked up more than twice. The list can be kept in the dictionary for easy access whenever they note that they have looked up the word more than twice. Many students enjoy their own personal spelling demon list.

APPENDIX

Words Often Spelled and Pronounced Incorrectly*

above	couple	give	machine	ranger	tongue
across	cousin	gives	many	ready	too
again	cruel	gloves	measure	really	touch
against	curve	gone	might	right	two
aisle		great	mild	rough	
already	dead	guard	million		use
another	deaf	guess	mind	said	usual
answer	debt	guest	minute	says	
anxious	desire	guide	mischief	school	vein
any	do		mother	science	very
	does	have	move	scissors	view
bar	done	head	Mr.	sew	
beautiful	don't	heart	Mrs.	shoe	was
beauty	double	heaven		should	wash
because	doubt	heavy	neighbor	sign	weather
been	dove	here	neither	snow	weight
behind	dozen	high	night	soften	were
believe			none	soldier	what
bind	early	idea		some	where
both	earn	Indian	ocean	someone	who
bough	eight	instead	of	someting	whom
bread	enough	isle	office	son	whose
bright	eye		often	soul	wild
brought	eyes	key	oh	special	wind
build		kind	once	spread	wolf
built	father	knee	one	square	woman
bury	fence	knew	onion	steak	women
busy	field	knife	only	straight	won
buy	fight	know	other	sure	would
	find		ought	sword	wrong
calf	folks	language			
captain	four	laugh	patient	their	you
caught	freight	laughed	piece	there	young
chief	friend	leather	pretty	they	your
child	front	library	pull	though	
clothes		light	purpose	thought	
colt	garage	lion	push	to	
coming	get	live	put	together	
cough	getting	lived		ton	
could	ghost	love	quiet		

*From Roach Van Allen. *Language Experiences in Communication*. Boston: Houghton Mifflin Company, 1976, p. 247.

List of Words for Spelling and Editing*

a	between	daddy	fellow	guess	is
about	big	dark	few		it
after	black	day	fifth	had	its
again	blue	dear	finally	hair	it's
all	body	did	find	half	
almost	book	didn't	fine	hand	jet
along	both	died	finished	happened	jump
alphabet	box	different	fire	happy	just
also	boy	do	first	hard	
always	bring	does	fish	has	keep
am	brother	dog	five	hat	kept
an	brown	done	fly	have	killed
and	but	don't	foot	having	kind
animal	buy	door	for	he	knew
another	by	down	found	head	know
any		drama	four	heard	
are	cafeteria	draw	fourth	help	language
around	call	dress	friend	her	large
art	came	drink	from	here	last
as	can		front	high	late
ask	can't	each	full	him	laugh
asked	car	early	fun	his	learned
at	cat	ears	funny	hit	leave
ate	chair	eat		hold	left
aunt	children	egg	game	home	legs
away	Christmas	eight	gave	hope	let
	city	end	get	hot	letter
baby	class	enough	getting	house	light
back	clean	even	girl	how	like
bad	close	ever	give	hundred	lips
ball	coat	every	giving	hurt	little
be	cold	everyone	glad		live
beautiful	come	everything	go	I	living
became	coming	eye	goes	ice	long
because	cook		good	if	look
bed	could	fall	got	I'll	lots
been	couldn't	far	grade	I'm	love
before	country	farm	gravel	important	
began	cow	fast	great	in	made
best	cut	father	green	interesting	make
better		feet	grow	into	man

*From Roach Van Allen. *Language Experiences in Communication*. Boston: Houghton Mifflin Company, 1976, pp. 248-49.

many	oh	rain	sometimes	time	went
may	old	ran	soon	to	where
me	on	read	spring	today	what
meet	once	reading	start	together	when
men	one	ready	stay	told	where
might	only	real	stop	tongue	which
milk	open	red	story	too	while
mine	or	rest	street	took	white
minutes	orange	ride	study	top	who
Miss	other	right	such	town	why
money	our	room	summer	tried	will
more	out	round	sun	trip	window
morning	outside	run	supper	try	winter
most	over		sure	turn	wish
mother	own	said	swim	two	with
mouth		same			without
Mr.	paint	saw	table	under	woman
Mrs.	painting	say	take	until	women
Ms.	paper	school	talk	up	won't
much	part	second	teacher	upon	wood
music	party	see	teeth	us	world
must	pass	seen	tell	use	would
my	past	send	ten	used	wouldn't
myself	pay	sent	than		write
	people	seven	thank	vacation	writing
name	person	shall	that	very	wrong
near	pet	she	the	visit	wrote
never	pick	should	their	vocabulary	
new	pig	show	them		yard
next	pink	sick	then	walk	year
nice	place	side	there	want	yellow
night	play	since	these	war	yes
no	please	sing	they	warm	yet
nobody	pretty	sister	thing	was	you
none	principal	sit	think	wash	young
north	pull	six	third	wasn't	your
not	purple	sixth	this	water	yours
now	put	sleep	those	way	
		small	thought	we	zipper
of	quick	so	three	weather	zoo
off	quiet	some	through	week	
often	quite	something	till	well	

List of 100 High-Frequency Words in Rank Order*

1. the	26. had	51. can	76. how
2. of	27. not	52. out	77. may
3. and	28. or	53. up	78. over
4. a	29. have	54. about	79. made
5. to	30. but	55. so	80. did
6. in	31. one	56. them	81. new
7. is	32. what	57. our	82. after
8. that	33. were	58. into	83. most
9. was	34. an	59. some	84. way
10. he	35. which	60. other	85. down
11. it	36. there	61. then	86. see
12. for	37. we	62. these	87. people
13. as	38. all	63. its	88. any
14. on	39. their	64. than	89. where
15. with	40. she	65. two	90. through
16. his	41. when	66. time	91. me
17. at	42. will	67. could	92. man
18. be	43. said	68. your	93. before
19. are	44. her	69. many	94. back
20. you	45. do	70. like	95. much
21. I	46. has	71. first	96. just
22. this	47. him	72. each	97. little
23. by	48. if	73. only	98. very
24. from	49. no	74. now	99. long
25. they	50. more	75. my	100. good

List of 300 High-Frequency Words**

a	always	at	best	brown	change
about	am	away	better	but	children
above	an		between	by	city
across	and	back	big		come
after	animal	be	black	called	could
again	another	because	blue	came	
air	any	been	book	can	day
all	are	before	both		days
almost	around	being	boy		did
also	as	below	boys		didn't

*From Roach Van Allen. *Language Experiences in Communication*. Boston: Houghton Mifflin Company, 1976, pp. 248-49.

**Ibid., pp. 218-19.

different
do
does
done
don't
down
draw
during

each
ears
end
enough
ever
example
eyes

far
feet
few
find
first
five
following
food
for
found
four
from
full

gave
get
girl
give
go
good
got
grade
great
green

had
hand
hard

has
have
he
head
hear
heard
help
her
here
high
him
his
home
house
how

I
if
important
in
into
is
it
its

just

keep
kind
knew
know

large
last
left
let
letter
life
light
like
line
little
long
look

looked

made
make
man
many
may
me
means
men
might
more
most
mother
Mr.
Mrs.
much
must
myself

name
need
never
new
next
night
no
not
now
number

of
off
old
on
once
one
only
open
or
other
others
our

out
outside
over
own

page
part
parts
party
people
picture
place
play
point
put

quiet

read
red
right
room
round
run

said
same
saw
school
second
see
sentence
set
several
she
should
show
side
since
small
so
some
something
soon
sound

start
still
stop
story
study
such

take
tell
than
that
the
their
them
then
there
these
they
thing
things
think
third
this
those
thought
three
through
time
times
to
today
together
told
too
took
top
toward
turned
two

under
until
up
us

use
used
using
usually

very

want
was
water
way
ways
we
week
well
went
were
what
when
where
which
while
white
who
whole
why
will
with
without
word
words
work
would
write

year
yellow
yes
you
your

List A: 350 Most Useful Spelling Words*

a	brought	eggs	hand	little	once
about	but	end	happy	live	one
across	buy	enjoyed	hard	long	or
after	by	every	has	look	other
afternoon			have	lot	our
again	call	far	he	lots	out
all	came	father	head	love	over
along	can	feet	heard		
always	candy	fifth	help	maybe	pair
am	car	find	her	make	paper
an	children	fine	here	making	party
and	Christmas	fire	high	man	people
another	class	first	him	many	picture
any	clean	fish	his	may	pictures
are	clothes	five	home	me	place
arithmetic	cold	flowers	hope	men	play
around	come	food	horse	might	played
as	comes	for	horses	milk	playing
at	coming	found	house	miss	please
aunt	corn	four	how	money	pretty
away	could	friend	hurt	more	program
	couldn't	friends		morning	put
	country	from	I	most	
baby	cousin	front	ice	mother	rain
back		funny	if	much	read
bad		game	I'm	my	reading
ball	daddy	games	in		red
be	day	gave	interesting	name	remember
because	days	get	into	near	ride
bed	dear	getting	is	never	right
been	did	girl	it	new	room
before	didn't	girls		next	run
best	dinner	give	just	nice	
better	do	glad		night	said
big	does	go	keep	no	Santa Claus
black	dog	goes	kind	not	saw
blue	doll	going	know	now	say
book	done	good			school
books	don't	got	last	o'clock	second
both	door	grade	left	of	see
box	down	ground	let	off	seen
boy	dress		letter	oh	set
boys			like	old	she
bring	each	had	liked	on	shoes
brother	eat	hair			

*From James A. Fitzgerald. *The Teaching of Spelling*. Milwaukee: Bruce Publishing Company, 1951, pp. 15-17.

should   street   there   tree   wants   winter

should	street	there	tree	wants	winter
show	summer	these	trees	was	wish
sister	Sunday	they	two	wash	with
six	supper	thing		water	won't
small	sure	things	under	way	work
snow		think	until	we	would
so	table	third	up	well	write
some	take	this	upon	went	writing
something	teacher	three	us	were	written
sometimes	teacher's	through	use	what	
soon	tell	time	used	when	year
spelling	ten	to		where	years
spring	thank	today	very	which	yes
started	that	together	visit	while	yesterday
stay	the	told		white	yet
stayed	their	too	walk	who	you
store	them	took	want	why	your
story	then	town	wanted	will	

List B: 450 Very Useful Spelling Words*

afraid	babies	brown	church	Dec.	egg
age	bank	build	city	December	eight
ago	barn	building	clay	decided	else
air	basket	built	close	deep	enjoy
airplane	bath	busy	coal	desk	enough
all right	beautiful		coat	died	even
almost	began	cake	color	different	evening
alone	behind	called	colors	dirt	ever
already	being	cannot	company	dishes	everybody
also	bet	can't	cook	doctor	everyone
animals	bicycle	card	corner	doesn't	everything
answer	bird	care	cotton	dogs	eyes
anything	birds	carry	course	doing	
apple	birthday	cars	cousins	dollars	face
apples	bit	cat	cow	draw	fair
April	board	catch	cows	dresses	fall
ask	boat	caught	cross	drink	family
asked	body	cave	cut	dry	farm
assembly	bottom	cents	cute	during	fast
are	bread	chair			fat
awful	breakfast	chicken	dad	early	Feb.
awhile	broke	chickens	dance	Easter	February
	brothers	child	dark	eating	feed

*From James A. Fitzgerald. *The Teaching of Spelling*. Milwaukee: Bruce Publishing Company, 1951, pp. 18-21.

feeling	hardly	lake	mouth	piece	seven
fell	hat	land	move	places	several
few	haven't	language	moved	plant	shall
field	having	large	Mr.	plays	shoot
fight	hay	largest	Mrs.	pony	short
finished	hear	late	mud	poor	sick
fishing	helped	later	music	present	side
flag	hill	laugh	must	presents	silk
flew	hit	lay	myself	P.S.	since
floor	hold	learn		pull	sing
flower	hole	learned	named		sisters
fly	hospital	leave	names	quite	sit
folks	hot	leaves	nearly		sitting
foot	houses	lessons	news	rabbit	skates
football	hundred	letters	nine	rabbits	skating
forest	hunt	light	north	radio	sled
forget	hunting	likes	nothing	raining	sleep
forgot	hurry	lines	Nov.	ran	snowing
fourth		lived	number	ready	soap
Friday	ice cream	lives	nuts	real	someone
fruit	I'll	living		received	sometime
full	important	looked	ocean	recess	song
fun	inches	looking	Oct.	rest	sorry
	Indian	looks	often	riding	south
garden	ink	lost	ones	ring	spend
geography	inside	lovely	only	river	stand
gets	instead	lunch	open	road	stars
gives	iron		orange	rode	state
glass	isn't	mad	oranges	roll	stick
gone	it's	mail	outside	rope	sticks
grades	its	makes	own	round	still
grandma	I've	mamma		rubber	stockings
grandmother		March	paint	running	stop
grass	Jan.	maybe	papa		stopped
great	jump	mean	park	same	stories
green		meat	part	sand	stove
grow	kept	meet	pass	sat	straight
guess	kill	merry	pen	Saturday	string
gun	killed	middle	pencil	says	strong
	kinds	mine	pet	sea	study
half	knew	minutes	piano	seat	studying
Halloween	knife	Miss	pick	sell	such
handkerchiefs		month	picnic	send	suit
hands	lady	mountains	pie	sent	sun

suppose	tells	tonight	uncle	week	word
surprised	test	top		weeks	words
sweet	than	toy	vacation	wet	working
swim	thanksgiving	train	valentine	wild	world
swimming	that's	tried	valentines	wind	wouldn't
	those	trip		window	wrote
takes	thought	truck	wagon	windows	
talk	throw	truly	warm	without	yard
tall	till	try	wasn't	women	yellow
teach	times	trying	watch	won	yours
teachers	tired	turn	wear	wood	
teeth	tomorrow	twenty	weather	woods	

BIBLIOGRAPHY

1. Calkins, Lucy M. *The Art of Teaching Writing*. Portsmouth, N.H.: Heinemann Educational Books, 1986.

2. Chomsky, Carol. "Reading, Writing, and Phonology." *Harvard Educational Review* 40 (May 1970): 287-309, 288.

3. Ibid., 303-305.

4. Davis, Lillie Smith. "The Applicability of Phonic Generalizations to Selected Spelling Programs." *Elementary English* 49, no. 5 (May 1972) 706-13.

5. Dolch, Edward W. *Better Spelling*. Champaign, Ill. Garrard Press, 1960.

6. Ferreiro, Emilia, and Teberosky, Ana. *Literacy Before Schooling*. Exeter, N.H.: Heinemann Educational Books, 1982.

7. Fitzgerald, James A. *A Basic Life Spelling Vocabulary*. Milwaukee: Bruce Publishing Company, 1951.

8. _____. "Research in Spelling and Handwriting." *Review of Educational Research* 22 (April 1952): 89-95.

9. Foran, Thomas G. *The Psychology and Teaching of Spelling*. Washington, D.C.: Catholic Education Press, 1934.

10. Graves, Donald H. *Writing: Teachers and Children at Work*. Portsmouth, N.H.: Heinemann Educational Books, 1983.

11. Henderson, Edmund H. *Teaching Spelling*. Boston: Houghton Mifflin Co., 1985.

12. Ibid., 41.

13. Ibid.

14. Horn, Ernest, *A Basic Writing Vocabulary*. Iowa City: University of Iowa Press, 1926.

15. _____. *Teaching Spelling*. Washington, D.C.: American Educational Research Association (1954): 17-18.

16. Horn, Thomas D. "Spelling." In *Encyclopedia of Educational Research*. Robert L. Ebel, ed. London: Macmillan Publishing Co. (1969): 1282-99, 1285.

17. _____. "Research in Spelling." *Elementary English* 37 (March 1960): 174-77.

18. _____. "The Effect of the Corrected Test on Learning to Spell." *Elementary School Journal* 47: (Janary 1947) 285.

19. _____, and Otto, Henry J. *Spelling Instruction: A Curriculum-Wide Approach*. Austin: Bureau of Laboratory School, 1954.

20. Jarvis, Oscar T. "How Much Time for Spelling?" *Instructor* 73 (September 1963): 594.

21. Moffett, James, and Wagner, Betty Jane. *Student-Centered Language Arts and Reading, K-13*. Boston: Houghton Mifflin Co., 1976.

22. Read, Charles. "Pre-School Children's Knowledge of English Phonology." *Harvard Educational Review* 39 (February 1971): 1-34.

23. Ibid.

24. Read, Edwin; Allred, Ruel A.; and Baird, Louise O. "Continuous Progress and Individualized Spelling Program." Provo, Utah: Unpublished paper, 1968.

25. Rinsland, Henry D. *A Basic Vocabulary of Elementary School Children*. New York: Macmillan Publishing Co., 1945.

26. Sherwin, J. Stephen. "Research and the Teaching of English." New York State English Council, December 1970.

27. Templeton, Shane. "The Circle Game of English Spelling: A Reappraisal for Teachers." *Language Arts* 56 (October 1979): 789-97, 795.

28. Tyler, Leona E. *The Psychology of Human Differences*. New York: Appleton-Century-Crofts, Inc., 1956.

29. Zuttell, Jerry. "Some Psycholinguistic Perspectives on Children's Spelling." *Language Arts* 55 (October 1978): 844-50, 848.

30. _____. "Some Psycholinguistic Perspectives on Children's Spelling." *Language Arts* 55 (October 1978): 844-50.

ANNOTATED BIBLIOGRAPHY

Allen, Roach Van. *Language Experiences in Communication*. Boston: Houghton Mifflin Co., 1976.
   Chapter on spelling explores spelling in writing and reading, functional spelling, linguistic factors that influence spelling, word lists for spelling and editing, and summarizes necessary skills and abilities.

Allred, Ruel A. *Spelling Trends, Content, and Methods*. Washington, D.C.: National Education Association, 1984.
   Gives classroom teachers current spelling trends including practices related to the writing process, ideas gained from studying the learner's perspective, and applications of computer-assisted instruction. In addition, the author reviews what to teach in spelling and how to teach it, and suggests several applications of spelling research.

Barbe, Walter B.; Francis, Azalia S.; and Braun, Lois A., eds. *Spelling: Basic Skills for Effective Communication*. Columbus, Ohio: Zaner-Bloser, 1982.
   Provides an overview of the research on spelling including diverse views on how children learn to spell. Also, a number of specific strategies are included.

Bissex, Glenda. *GYNS AT WRK: A Child Learns to Write and Read*. Cambridge, Mass.: Harvard University Press, 1980.
   Explains the writing development of one child. Insight can be gained about writing and reading development by reading this carefully done case study on the author's own son.

Boyd, Gertrude A., and Talbert, E. Gene. *Spelling in the Elementary School*. Columbus, Ohio: Charles E. Merrill Publishing Co., 1971.
   Reviews the history of spelling, including factors in learning to spell, reasons for inability to spell, and individual differences in spelling. Suggests several activities and games for teaching spelling.

Burling, Robbins. *English in Black and White*. New York: Holt, Rinehart and Winston, 1973.
   Several pages on spelling relate problems and solutions in the area of dialects and spelling, and briefly discuss regularized spelling.

Calkins, Lucy M. *The Art of Teaching Writing*. Portsmouth, N.H.: Heinemann Educational Books, 1986.
   Presents ideas about teaching writing, including specific suggestions for each grade level from kindergarten through early adolescence. The author

also discusses reading and writing relationships along with writing across the curriculum.

Dolch, Edward W. *Better Spelling*. Champaign, Ill.: Garrard Press, 1960.
Discusses words to teach, spelling period, spelling generalizations, and attitudes and habits in learning to spell. Appendix lists the 2,000 commonest spelling words.

Donoghue, Mildred R. *The Child and the English Language Arts*. Dubuque, Iowa: William C. Brown Co., 1979.
Chapter on spelling contains information about psychology of spelling, invented spelling, and individualized spelling, as well as suggestions for several spelling games.

Ferreira, Nelly Ceres. "Spelling and Handwriting." In *Classroom-Relevant Research in the Language Arts*, pp. 119-25. Washington, D.C.: Association for Supervision and Curriculum Development, 1978.
Provides a brief review of spelling research (particularly in the seventies), suggestions for improving the teaching of spelling, and miscellaneous comments on spelling.

Ferreiro, Emilia, and Teberosky, Ana. *Literacy Before Schooling*. Exeter, N.H.: Heinemann Educational Books, 1982.
Shows how children construct a written language system, using a Piagetian approach for studying children's literacy development. The authors present an entire chapter on the evolution of writing.

Fitzgerald, James A. *A Basic Life Spelling Vocabulary*. Milwaukee: Bruce Publishing Co., 1951.
Provides 2,650 words most frequently used in child and adult writing, together with suggestions for their use and an especially informative discussion about grade placement of words. Text should be helpful to teachers developing their own graded word lists.

Fitzgerald, James A. *The Teaching of Spelling*. Milwaukee: Bruce Publishing Co., 1951.
Suggests methods for teaching spelling and selecting words to study, as well as several activities for learning to spell.

Frith, Uta, ed. *Cognitive Processes in Spelling*. New York: Academic Press, 1980.
Includes spelling ideas and research of various contributors categorized into several areas: spelling instruction and reforms, spelling and language, orthographic awareness, spelling and word recognition, spelling strategies, spelling errors, spelling and development, spelling and language disorders, and spelling and dyslexia. Also considers historical, linguistic, and cognitive approaches.

Graves, Donald H. *Writing: Teachers and Children at Work*. Portsmouth, N.H.: Heinemann Educational Books, 1983.
Includes a chapter on spelling within the framework of the writing process. Gives a brief discussion of invented spelling and suggests strategies to improve poor spelling.

Henderson, Edmund H., and Beers, James W., eds. *Developmental and Cognitive Aspects of Learning to Spell*. Newark, Del.: International Reading Association, 1980.
Contains chapters on such topics as dialect and spelling, relationship of cognitive development to spelling and reading abilities, and three steps to teaching beginning readers to spell.

Henderson, Edmund H. *Learning to Read and Spell*. Dekalb, Ill.: Northern Illinois University Press, 1981.
Provides ideas about reading and spelling, including several specific sections about spelling. Spelling topics include historical perspective, spelling regularities, invented spelling, and stages of spelling.

Henderson, Edmund H. *Teaching Spelling*. Boston: Houghton Mifflin Co., 1985.
Reviews the history of English spelling. The author presents a developmental approach to teaching children to spell with specific suggestions at all elementary grade levels.

Hildreth, Gertrude. *Teaching Spelling*. New York: Henry Holt and Co., 1955.
Provides an overview of the teaching of spelling with interesting chapters on the principles of learning applied to spelling, and the beginnings of spelling. Contains a vocabulary list of 2,996 words with teaching suggestions and directions for dividing the total list into graded lists.

Horn, Ernest. *A Basic Writing Vocabulary*. Iowa City: University of Iowa Press, 1926.
Reviews previous spelling vocabulary studies and describes the author's investigation. Includes list of 10,000 words most commonly used in adult writing, as well as discussion and evaluation.

Moffett, James, and Wagner, Betty Jane. *Student-Centered Language Arts and Reading, K-13*. Boston: Houghton Mifflin Co., 1976.
Several sections offer spelling ideas involving phonics, games, and proofreading, as well as ways to improve spelling.

Peters, Margaret L. *Spelling: Caught or Taught?* New York: Humanities Press, 1967.
Discusses the spelling problem, determinants of competence in spelling, approaches to teaching spelling, and assessment of spelling.

Rinsland, Henry D. *A Basic Vocabulary of Elementary School Children*. New York: Macmillan Publishing Co., 1945.

Provides ideas about a basic vocabulary including the need for studying vocabularies, sources of material, uses of the word list, and variations in occurrence of words. Also includes the author's word list.

Robinson, H. Alan, and Burrows, Alvina Treut. *Teacher Effectiveness in Elementary Language Arts: A Progress Report*. Urbana, Ill.: Clearinghouse on Reading and Communication Skills, 1974.

Section entitled "Teaching Behaviors in Spelling Instruction: Report of the Literature Search" concludes there has been no research to determine the effects of teaching behaviors upon spelling achievement of students.

Smith, E. Brooks; Goodman, Kenneth S.; and Meredith, Robert. *Language and Thinking in the Elementary School*. New York: Holt, Rinehart and Winston, 1970.

Several pages of this work discuss new views about spelling, spelling in context, and dialects and spelling.

Stauffer, Russell G. *The Language-Experience Approach to the Teaching of Reading*. New York: Harper and Row, Publishers, 1970.

Several pages devoted to spelling in a language-experience approach consider basic principles, formal instruction, phonological development, research, and spelling consciousness.